Deb's book

Illustrated by Nina O'Connell

The race page 2

The red house page 7

Up and down page 12

Macmillan Education

The race

Can you run fast,
said Deb the rat.
Let's have a race.

I can run fast,
said Ben the dog.
But Fat Pig can't.

I can run fast,
said Jip the cat.
But Fat Pig can't.

I can run fast,
said Sam the fox.
But Fat Pig can't.

I can run fast,
said Fat Pig.
Look at me.

The red house

I have a pot of
red paint, said Deb.
I want a red house.
But I am small and
the house is tall.

I will help you, said Meg.
But I am small and
the house is tall.

I will help you, said Ben.

But I am small and

the house is tall.

I will help you, said Sam.
I am tall.

Your house is red and we are red.

Up and down

Get on the see-saw Meg,
said Fat Pig.
It will go up and down.

Meg got on the see-saw.
It did not go up and down.

Get on the see-saw Jip,

said Fat Pig.

It will go up and down.

But it did not go up and down.

Get on the see-saw Ben,

said Fat Pig.

It will go up and down.

But it did not go up and down.

Get on the see-saw Deb,
said Fat Pig.
It will go up and down.
Deb got on the see-saw.
It went up and down.